# WHERE DOES THE MOON GO?

A Question of Science Book

# WHERE DOES THE MOON GO?

by Sidney Rosen
illustrated by Dean Lindberg

Carolrhoda Books, Inc. / Minneapolis

Each word that appears in **BOLD** in the text is explained in the glossary on page 40.

Text copyright © 1992 by Sidney Rosen
Illustrations copyright © 1992 by Carolrhoda Books, Inc.
Photographs reproduced courtesy of: cover, pp. 2-3, © David Falconer; pp. 5, 9, 13-17, 20, NASA; pp. 6-7, 29, California Institute of Technology; pp. 18-19, Jim Simondet; pp. 30, 32-37, Lick Observatory; pp. 38-39, NOAO.

LIBRARY OF CONGRESS CATALOGING-IN-PUBLICATION DATA

Rosen, Sidney.
   Where does the moon go? / by Sidney Rosen ; with illustrations by Dean Lindberg.
      p.   cm. — (A Question of science)
   Summary: Follows the moon through its twenty-eight-day trip around the Earth and identifies its different phases.
   ISBN 0-87614-685-X (lib. bdg.)
   1. Moon—Juvenile literature. 2. Moon—Phases—Juvenile literature. [1. Moon.] I. Lindberg, Dean, ill. II. Title. III. Series.
QB582.R67 1992
523.3'2—dc20                                                        91-16069
                                                                         CIP
                                                                          AC

Manufactured in the United States of America

1 2 3 4 5 6 7 8 9 10 01 00 99 98 97 96 95 94 93 92

Will the moon be up in the sky tonight?

If it's a nice, clear night, look outside and see.
No moon in the sky? Maybe some nights the moon just
goes away. Or does it? To find out where the moon
goes, you have to ask a lot of questions. So, fire away!

*Okay, first question.  What is the moon?*
*Is it a planet like Mars and Jupiter?*

No, a moon is the **satellite** of a planet.  A satellite is a smaller object that goes around a larger object in space.  Our moon circles the planet Earth as though it were a balloon tied to Earth by a big, stretched-out rubber band.

*Can we see the rubber band that holds the moon to the Earth?*

No, it's an invisible force.  But even if you can't see it, it has a name: **gravity**.

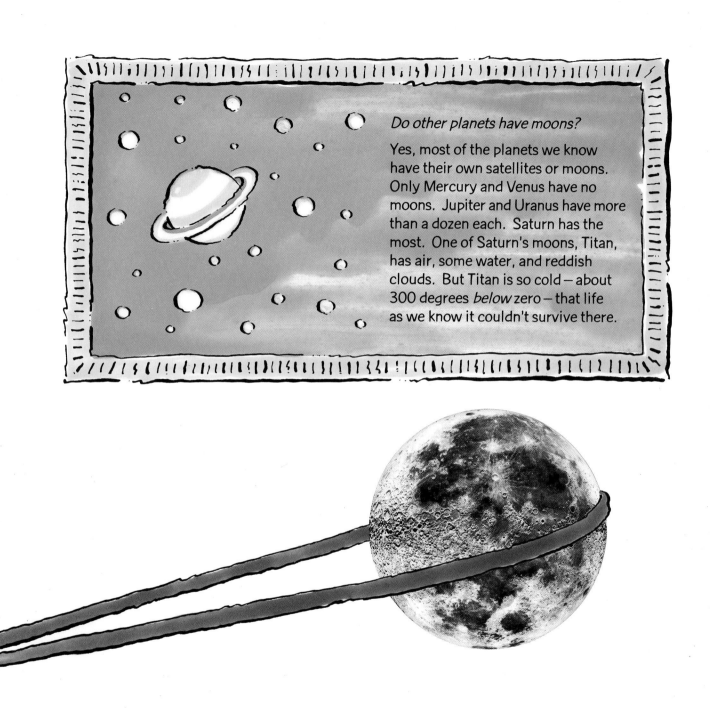

### Do other planets have moons?

Yes, most of the planets we know have their own satellites or moons. Only Mercury and Venus have no moons. Jupiter and Uranus have more than a dozen each. Saturn has the most. One of Saturn's moons, Titan, has air, some water, and reddish clouds. But Titan is so cold — about 300 degrees *below* zero — that life as we know it couldn't survive there.

## What does gravity do?

Gravity keeps the moon moving around the Earth in a path called an **orbit**. If you drew a line along the moon's orbit, it would look like a circle that is a little bit squashed. Gravity keeps the moon from leaving its orbit.

*So the moon can't float away because of gravity?*

That's right.  Dogs and cats and boats can't get away
from Earth, either.  Gravity keeps us stuck to the Earth,
too.  Just try jumping straight up.  No matter how high
you jump, you always come right back to Earth.

*But what about birds?  And airplanes?  They sure
get away from Earth.*

True. By using their wings, birds can move against the pull of gravity. But it took people a long time to figure out how to do what birds do naturally.

*But birds and airplanes still can't fly to outer space, can they?*

No, you need a rocket ship to get away from the pull
of Earth's gravity. Using a rocket ship that traveled at
25,000 miles per hour, people have even visited
the moon.

**What is it like on the moon?**

*Are there footprints on the moon?*

On July 20, 1969, the first human being stood on the moon. Neil Armstrong came down the little ladder from the *Apollo 11* Landing Module. Because there are no winds or rain on the moon, Neil Armstrong's footprints can still be seen today, along with those of other astronauts.

It's like a desert, with sand and mountains and **craters**. There is no air to breathe, so **astronauts** carried their own air. They found no signs of life there.

*Can you see the Earth from the moon?*

Sure.  You can see blue oceans, white clouds, and patches of land.  You can even see the Earth turning or rotating slowly.  This **rotation** causes night and day on Earth.

*How does that work?*

Each morning, the Earth turns so that you face the Sun. On your part of the planet, it's daytime. Slowly— so slowly you can't feel it—the Earth turns some more. Soon it has turned so much that you face away from the Sun. Night is coming on.

As the Earth rotates, it also orbits the Sun. While one band of gravity keeps the moon going around the Earth, another one keeps the Earth going around the Sun. The Earth is a satellite of the Sun.

*Which satellite takes longer to go around on its orbit once, the Earth or the moon?*

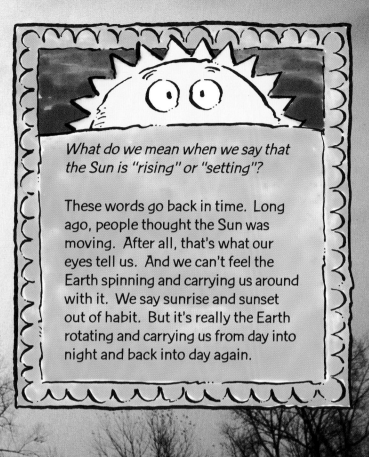

*What do we mean when we say that the Sun is "rising" or "setting"?*

These words go back in time. Long ago, people thought the Sun was moving. After all, that's what our eyes tell us. And we can't feel the Earth spinning and carrying us around with it. We say sunrise and sunset out of habit. But it's really the Earth rotating and carrying us from day into night and back into day again.

It takes our planet about 365 days, or one year, to go around the Sun once. In that time, the moon goes around the Earth about 12 times. But as the moon moves around the Earth, we only see one side of it.

*You mean that we always see the same side of the moon?*

That's right.  The side we see is called the **near side**.
It always faces the Earth.  The side we never see is called
the **far side**.  It always faces away from Earth.

*Then the moon must not turn like the Earth does
or we would see the other side, right?*

*Who first saw the far side of the moon?*

In 1959, the Soviet Union shot a rocket ship, *Luna 2*, as far as the moon. Their next ship, *Luna 3*, sent back pictures of the moon's far side. Before *Luna 3*, no one had ever seen the far side of the moon. The moon's far side has more craters than the side that faces Earth. Scientists still don't know why this is so.

**Don't be so sure. Try this and then decide. First, take a ball and mark one side with an *X*. The ball will be your moon. The *X* will be a landmark—maybe a huge crater on the near side of the moon.**

Take your moon and hold it over any one
of the eight spots around the Earth in
this picture. Turn the ball so the *X*
faces the Earth. Move your ball
from one spot to the next. Make
sure that the mark on the ball
stays facing the Earth.

*So what will I see?*

NIGHT

ZZZZZZZ

THE

Just like the moon in space,
your ball has to rotate,
or the *X* will not always face Earth.

By the time you take the moon on one
trip around the Earth, the ball will
make one full rotation.
And the same side will
always be facing the Earth.

WOOF!!!

DAY

EARTH

*But if we always see the same side of
the moon, then why does the moon look
different on different nights?*

What do you mean by different?

Sometimes we see a round moon
like a fifty-cent piece,

sometimes a half-moon like a slice of melon.

And sometimes the moon looks like the top of
a thumbnail. What are all these shapes?

**If the Sun isn't out at night, then how does sunlight get to the moon?**

At night, the Sun shines on the other side of the Earth. But some of the sunlight goes past Earth. That sunlight bounces off the moon, the same way light bounces off a mirror. Try shining a flashlight at any mirror in your house. See what happens? The light shines right back into your eyes. The moon is like that mirror, and the Sun is like your flashlight. That is how we can see the moon shining at night.

The flashlight is the Sun, the mirror is the moon, and the globe is the Earth.

The different shapes are called **phases**. The shapes we see are made by the Sun's light as it falls on the moon.

*Then do I see a full moon instead of a half-moon because more sunlight hits the moon?*

No, the same amount of sunlight always hits the moon. But the moon doesn't stay in the same place for long. From the Earth, we see first more and more, then less and less, of the moon's near side lit up by sunlight during the moon's round trip.

*Where would a person have to be on Earth to see all the different phases of the moon?*

Just where you are now.

In its first phase, the moon is between the Earth and the Sun.  This phase is called a **new moon**.

*What does a new moon look like?*

Nothing at all! We can't see the new moon. It's hidden in the strong light of the Sun.

*Can I see the new moon at night when the Sun isn't shining?*

No, that's not possible. Remember, during the new moon, the moon is between the Earth and the Sun. So when it is night on Earth, you would be facing away from both the Sun and the moon.

*Then when will I see the moon?*

You will see it a day or so after the new moon. This phase of the moon is called a **waxing crescent**.

Waxing means that the moon is getting bigger. It's called a crescent because it is shaped like a backward *C* or a crescent roll. You will see the moon first in the daytime sky. Only during the day, the moon doesn't look yellow, like it does at night. It looks white, like a ghost.

I'm too scared to look!

*When will I see the other phases of the moon?*

## When is a quarter a half?

Some people say I'm a quarter!

Some people say I'm a half!

The half-moon we see seven days after the new moon is often called the first quarter moon. The moon has completed the first quarter of its four-week-long trip around the Earth. We sometimes call this phase a half-moon, because we can see one half of the near side of the moon lit up by the Sun.

Seven days after a new moon, you will be able to see a white half-moon rising. As the Earth whirls you into night, the half-moon will begin to shine with a yellow light.

A few days later, you will see even more of the moon.

Fourteen days after the new moon, you will see a full moon. The full moon rises just as you are moving into night. The moon only *looks* as if it has grown. What really changes is how much of the moon we can see.

Several nights after the full moon, you will see this much of the moon. Now the moon looks like it's shrinking.

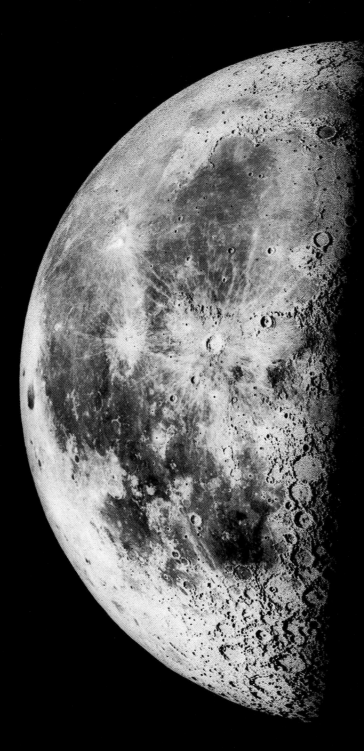

Seven days after the full moon, there will be another half-moon. But chances are, you will be fast asleep in bed. This half-moon rises after midnight. After you wake up, you may see the half-moon setting.

A few days more, and you will see another C-shaped moon. It's called a **waning crescent**. Waning means it's getting smaller.

Then, about 28 days after the moon started its trip around Earth, even that thumbnail of light will be gone. It's time for a new moon again.

*So, if I don't see the moon at night, where did it go?*

'Don't worry. It hasn't broken away from Earth's gravity or floated out into space. The moon is somewhere else on its trip around the Earth. When you can't see it, perhaps another young person in a different part of the world is looking at it.

And that's where the moon has gone!

# GLOSSARY

**astronauts:** People who travel in space, beyond the Earth

**craters:** Circle-shaped hollows of different sizes on the moon's surface, probably caused by meteors or comets crashing into the moon

**far side:** The side of the moon that always faces away from Earth

**gravity:** The force that makes objects attract each other. The Earth's gravity is so strong it keeps us stuck to Earth.

**near side:** The side of the moon that always faces the Earth

**new moon:** The phase of the moon that occurs when the moon lies exactly between the Sun and the Earth. A new moon cannot be seen from Earth.

**orbit:** The path of one object around another, such as the moon around the Earth

**phases:** The monthly changes in the appearance of the moon as seen from Earth

**rotation:** The turning of any body around its own center. The Earth turns, or rotates, on its axis (the imaginary line that goes through the Earth from the North Pole to the South Pole).

**satellite:** An object that is moving around a larger body, such as the moon moving around the Earth

**waning crescent:** The phase of the moon that occurs just *before* a new moon

**waxing crescent:** The phase of the moon that occurs just *after* a new moon